The Contractor's 60 Minute Exit Plan

How to Cash Out, Eliminate Taxes and Retire Comfortably

Written by a Contractor for a Contractor

Beacon Exit Planning

Joe Bazzano and Kevin Kennedy

1st edition
Print ISBN: 9781719879149

Dedication

My life took a new path in 1980 when I was hired by my business mentor Richard Evans to join his private specialty contracting company after leaving an eleven-year career in education.

Dick was a master teacher, a respected business and community leader who led by example. He created a business culture dedicated the customer, guided by integrity and focused on safety and quality.

In 1986 he approached our management team to buy the company from him over a 10-year period with a management buyout.

His guidance prepared us for an exhilarating experience that led us on a path of personal growth, managerial excellence, ownership and leadership. During this succession he allowed the team to grow through our mistakes, stretch our capabilities, and work collectively for our company's mutual success.

During this period, we also observed a change in Dick's leadership style as he gradually relinquished control and became our advisor, coach and mentor. His hands-off management style was a new experience for Dick and for us.

He recognized that his legacy and corporate responsibility was to move our management team into leadership and create a business with sustainable earnings without his presence.

Dick Evans blessed my life and many others. His presence and example created a benchmark for me to reach in my business and personal life. I am forever thankful and blessed that this true gentleman came into my life and business.

—Kevin Kennedy

Table of Contents

Preface

The goal of The Contractor's 60-Minute Exit Plan is for you, the contractor owner, to walk away with a clearer picture of the challenging process you will face in the exit process. It is intended to make the complex understandable, so you can envision the key considerations, risks and processes of exit planning.

This book is not intended to make you an exit planner, but to help you to envision the path that you are about to take for your exit and financial independence. In other words, the intent is to teach you how to tell time, not how to build a watch.

This book is co-authored by Kevin Kennedy and Joe Bazzano of Beacon Exit Planning. The authors complement each other with their background, experiences and education. Kennedy offers expertise and takeaways based on his first-hand experience of buying and selling a specialty trade contracting business. Bazzano brings a more technical approach, based on his education, background and certification as a professional adviser.

Confidentiality

The case studies and anecdotes included in the book are based on real-life experiences. All customer information is confidential, and personal information has been redacted to protect their identity.

Disclaimer

The content of this book is intended to be educational material based on the experiences of the authors. The book does not constitute, nor is it intended to be, personal financial advice nor corporate legal, accounting, insurance, investment or tax advice. Business owners should consult their specialty adviser for personalized exit advice.

An owner's strategy should be based on their own personal and business situation, and the content of this book should not be taken out of context. The book should be used as an educational guide to help owners understand the opportunities and potential pitfalls that a contractor may experience during this very important process.

Information provided herein has been obtained from the authors' experience providing guidance to exiting owners. Beacon Exit Planning makes no guarantees, express or implied, as to the accuracy or completeness thereof.

U.S. Treasury Circular 230 requires that this firm advise you that any tax advice provided was not intended or written to be used, and cannot be used by you, for the purpose of avoiding penalties that the IRS could impose upon you.

Consult your attorneys, tax professionals for each specific situation based on you, your business, your state, local and federal laws.

Introduction

—By Kevin Kennedy

"You don't know, what you don't know."

While every business owner's exit from their company will be unique, each exit will be challenging, the stakes will be high, and the odds will be against success.

Consider, around 70 percent of your wealth is trapped inside your illiquid business. In your exit, you will need to find a way to retire and not run out of money.

But the odds aren't on your side. According to the Family Firm Institute Inc., fewer than 30 percent of private companies ever sell or transfer to the second generation. Further, 90 percent of those companies fail transfer to the third generation.

For companies looking to sell their business to an outside buyer, the statistics are similarly daunting. Fewer than 20 percent of the companies that go to market actually sell, according to the U.S. Chamber of Commerce.

If you are one of the lucky owners who cash out, you are guaranteed that Uncle Sam will be waiting there to collect his "fair share." Taxes can range from 0-to-55 percent, depending on the exit path and tax strategies.

Simply put, you would be naïve to think exiting a business is a cake walk. The odds are simply against you selling and transferring your company.

I personally faced this difficult truth head on. I was part of a management team that became the third generation of owners of a specialty contracting company. During our tenure at the company, we grew with the business from a family business employing approximately 40 associates to a mature self-sustaining company employing over 200 associates and nationally ranked as one of the Top 20 Engineering News-Record Specialty Contractors in the United States. At the end of our careers we were prepared to pass the reigns to the new ownership team, as they were anxious to take the reins.

We were ready to exit the business. But, our efforts to choose the right strategy for monetizing our business came at a cost. We spent an excess of seven years and over $250,000 evaluating each exit path reacting to opportunities and options, instead of having an adviser who could map this out for us.

We spent three years processing two solid offers from industry consolidators. Each included a time-consuming and grueling due diligence process with the cycle of emotion. And each distracted us from running our growing business.

We worked with a questionable mergers and acquisitions adviser who gave us an expensive valuation and a low outside offer. And we also sought input from an employee stock ownership plan advisor.

In the end, we determined that a management buyout was the best option for our company. We focused on succession and identifying our next leadership team to sell our company internally. The three owners signed an agreement in 2003 for a 10-year buyout to five other managers and we, the owners, retired over the next three to five years.

In retrospect, we could see that the process was a distraction and a waste of considerable time, money and resources. While we successfully transitioned the business, it wasn't easy. The path is not straight and narrow and at times bumpy. And, we made some key mistakes along the way, which are outlined in the last chapter of this book.

Our biggest mistake was coming in without an exit strategy. We didn't understand our options, values, taxes or risk. We three owners came in with three different goals and time lines. And, amid the booming economy, we were reactionary, responding to potential options without any internal direction, plan or independent professional advice.

Additionally, we thought we could do it ourselves. We were confident, independent businessmen. But we were rookies in our first rodeo when it came to exiting the business. We did not understand the true risk of the exit process. We underestimated the challenge of juggling and coordinating the messaging and advice from all the different adviser towers.

Throughout the process, we had good, but not great, advice. We now know we received general advice by advisers who were not specialized in business transactions. I later discovered that this cookie cutter advice cost our company, the buyers and our exiting owners millions of dollars in unnecessary taxes.

Yes, we left a lot on the table, but still very fortunate to achieve our financial and legacy goals. I also do not harbor any ill feeling toward our advisers as they were ethical, but not specialized or educated in the *advanced* techniques and exit strategies to reduce the owner's financial risk.

They simply did not know what they didn't know.

I learned a lot from our rocky exit, and after retirement I went back to school for two years to become certified planner as other owners were requesting my help.

This experience has become the motivation for my articles, presentations and writing of this book. I wake every day wanting to help other owners avoid my mistakes.

Chapter 1: There's Only One Guarantee

There are no guarantees in owning and managing your business, except one: you will eventually exit. Whether you exit voluntarily or involuntarily, the day will come when you will say goodbye. To ensure that your inevitable exit is a successful one—an exit that will deliver on your future financial, personal and business goals—you need an exit plan.

This chapter introduces the multi-faceted exit planning process, from valuation to succession planning, and presents the transfer options available to contractor owners. It also takes a closer look at the risks, challenges and stakes involved in a business exit.

The stakes

What prompts an owner's exit? In the best scenarios, an owner will choose voluntarily to depart the business, perhaps to enter retirement or start a new venture. An owner also might be confronted with a forced or involuntary departure from the business due to death, disability or divorce. No matter the reason for an exit, planning for the inevitable is essential. The stakes are too high to ignore.

Numerous people depend on a business as a source of economic benefit, beginning with the owner and the owner's family. Statistically speaking, an estimated 75 percent of a business owner's wealth is trapped in their non-liquid business, according to estimates from PricewaterhouseCoopers. At Beacon Exit Planning, we have encountered many customers whose percentage of wealth in the business is much higher—in some cases as high as 92 percent. The primary reason for planning is to provide the owner with financial security to protect that wealth.

The exit plan also seeks to protect the other parties who rely on the business, such as employees and their families. In some cases, the business' reach might extend even farther. Perhaps a community depends on a business for financial support.

To ensure a successful exit that continues to meet the needs of the owner, the family and the employees, an owner must find a way to transfer the business to a new generation.

Transfer options

A contractor owner will have several options to transition a business to new ownership. Voluntarily, the business owner can sell to a strategic or investment-minded buyer, or the seller can transition the business to employees, family members or key members of the organization. Because of the inherent characteristics of a construction company, the transaction typically involves a sale to family members or employees. This is called an internal sale.

External sales—either to strategic buyers or investment firms—are less common in the construction industry. Construction companies are hard to sell. Outside buyers typically see too much risk. Unless the owner has structured the company in a way that generates quality cash flows, the most likely buyer to see value in a contracting firm will be someone who already works for the business.

Other transfer options include gifting and an employee stock ownership plan, or ESOP. Gifting, generally an option for family businesses, is not a monetary transaction, but is used more as an efficient way to transfer wealth between family and generations. Meanwhile, an ESOP is essentially a retirement plan where the plan trust buys corporate stock as opposed to other marketable securities typically found in more traditional retirement plans, such as profit sharing and 401(k) plans. Because the trust operates for the benefit of the employees' retirement, the ESOP qualifies under the Employee Retirement Income Securities Act or ERISA and is under the oversight of the Department of Labor and the Internal Revenue Service. An ESOP can be a very tax efficient tool for exiting a business.

The exit plan

Transitioning the ownership and management of a company to new ownership, whether from inside or outside of the business, is challenging and can take years to complete. Exit planning will help an exiting owner implement strategies that will increase the odds of success.

The exit plan asks an owner to outline their future financial goals of the transaction. This generally involves the owner finding a way to monetize the business so they can replace their income once they leave the business.

The plan also asks an owner to look at their future personal goals and their future goals for the business. In other words, what will the owner do, and what will happen to the company, once the owner has departed?

A properly written exit plan should not stop there. A properly drafted exit plan should include strategies and tools to manage financial risk. It should coordinate the owner's goals with the necessary legal documents and protect the business from unintended consequences such as predatory lawsuits or economic downturns.

An owner also must consider the various disciplines that go into the exiting process. During execution of an exit, a typical team will consist of corporate attorney, estate planning attorneys, accountants, financial planners, life insurance agents and business appraisers. If an owner is looking to transition with some sort of specialty area such as an ESOP, he or she may need additional advisors such as ESOP attorneys or business brokers or investment bankers. Without a plan, this can become quite expensive for the exiting owner.

Exit planning can take about six months to a year or more to put into action.

The pitfalls of exiting

Exiting a business presents numerous pitfalls and challenges. Most owners—70 percent—don't manage to successfully transition the business to new ownership. The question then becomes: Why is it so hard to transition a business?

Several key issues make exiting a business difficult: valuation, taxation, succession and contingency planning.

Business value. What is the value of the business and how is it set? The business valuation world is complex, and a qualified business appraiser should be utilized to assist the owner in determining the value. A business can have several different values associated with it depending on the exit method selected, the ownership interest being sold and economic climate the business operates. The business owner should understand the nuances of business value, including what adds value and what detracts value from the business.

Business owners often have unrealistic expectation of what the company is worth. In the valuation world remember one thing; the business is only worth what someone is willing to pay for it. It is incumbent on the owner to make it saleable.

Tax planning. Business owners are familiar with consulting accountants to determine the potential tax obligation on the upcoming profits for the year. Some business owners may also have a plan for estate tax. But how many have actually run through the process of identifying the various exiting alternatives and studying the tax ramifications when selling the business?

The tax liabilities vary greatly depending on the type of exit an owner pursues. In certain instances, the effective tax rate in the sale of a business could exceed 50 percent. That would mean the government would get more than the owner in the transaction.

Exit planning can help owners better understand the taxation associated with each type of transfer and make better financial decisions during their exit.

Succession planning. The process of succession planning involves training key individuals within a company to eventually replace the owner. This is an often-overlooked process until it's too late. A succession plan deals with changing behaviors and attitudes in the business. This process can take from two years to 10 years depending on the level of planning that has already been employed.

Neglecting to plan for business succession can affect an owner's ability to successfully exit their business. For example, if an owner is selling to an outside party, the buyer wants to know that a well-seasoned management team is in place to help support operations into the future. Not having this management team in place makes the business less attractive to buyers.

The lack of a strong succession plan can also negatively affect an internal transfer. For example, transferring ownership to a management team, generally requires that the management team gradually payout the exiting owner over time. In other words, the ability for the owner to get paid relies on the ability of the management team to continue to run the business successfully. An exiting owner wants to make sure the check clears the bank, and this requires a capable and well-trained management team.

Contingency planning. The final common pitfall involves missteps in contingency planning, primarily improperly documented buy/sell agreements or improperly designated life insurance policies.

These two items go hand in hand and are dependent on each other for proper utilization.

A buy/sell agreement is an agreement between existing shareholders that outlines the terms of a buyout in the event of several triggering events, such as death, disability divorce, and both voluntary and involuntary departure for cause. It should be drafted in a form that supports the owners' intentions and leaves very little ambiguity in what is most often very difficult times.

The life insurance is often used as the funding mechanism for the buy/sell agreement. If not properly owned, or if the beneficiary is not properly designated, it could create a situation where a significant tax benefit is missed.

Exit planners

Managing the exit planning and execution process is critical in achieving success. All too often, advisors promote a one size fits all approach to the process without considering the owner's ultimate goals or considering other aspects of planning in the business owner's world. An exit planner, on the other hand, can assist a business owner in organizing and consulting the business owner on the various strategies available to them.

Think of an exit planner like an architect. An architect must know and understand the various disciplines that go into building a house or structure. He or she must understand the specifications of an electrician, plumber, carpenter and roofer and integrate the various disciplines in a comprehensive easy to follow blue print so that the contractors can identify, evaluate and execute.

An exit planner works much in the same way during an owner's exit. The exit planner understands tax, accounting, valuation, financial planning and to some extent legal issues that confront a business owner during this process. From that knowledge, the planner can create a comprehensive plan that can be the source for the owner's exiting strategy.

In addition, the exit planner should have a thorough knowledge of the various disciplines that are incorporated into the plan. It is not only important that the exit planner guide and direct the process for the owner, but it is critical that the planner can evaluate and discuss key issues with other advisors on the team.

The next chapter of this book will discuss the beginning of the exit planning process, offering additional information on setting goals. It will also take owners through Beacon Exit Planning's comprehensive exit planning process, from discovery to design.

BONUS ARTICLE

How to Retire by Replacing Your Income & Yourself

Leaving any business that you've spent a career—and in many cases a lifetime—building into a provider for your family and the families of those employees that helped along the way can be a challenge, to say the least.

The article is an interview by a magazine editor before a national presentation at an industry trade show that will give you further understanding of the owners three large obstacles: taxes, succession and determining the answer to the question "What do I do in retirement?"

Link: http://beaconexitplanning.com/bookbonuses/

Notes

Chapter 2: Begin the Planning Process

Exiting your business and monetizing your largest single asset will be complex, strenuous, emotional and potentially very expensive. As emphasized in the previous chapter, a customized and comprehensive exit plan will provide you with much of the relevant information in a format that is organized and provides alternative strategies.

This chapter will help you to start the exit planning process, beginning with your business, personal and financial goals. It will present a structure for owners looking to exit their business and shed light on the common myths and misconceptions about exiting that could derail the process. Owners who come into the exit process carrying any of these misconceptions are getting off track before they even begin.

Exit myths and misconceptions

During conversations with hundreds of successful business owners, we have discovered some common misconceptions about exiting their businesses and harvesting the estimated **75 percent** of their wealth that is trapped in their illiquid business. If an owner does not understand the following myths, they are probably putting their wealth at risk.

"I will just sell my business and retire."

In reality, fewer than 20 percent of all businesses taken to market for sale close, according to statistics from the U.S. Chamber of Commerce. Because of the inherent nature of the construction industry, with greater market variability and higher risks, the closing rate to an outside seller is even smaller, at about 10 percent, according to the FMI, the Fails Management Institute. Owners that do sell to an outside party are generally successful because the company operates in a unique niche or location, and during a strong economy.

"I will deal with my exit plan in five years."

I will talk to a business owner about when he or she intends to retire, and the answer is usually a predictable: "in five years." Three years later when asked the same question, the answer is still, "in five years." In these cases, the owner has no plan and is not mentally prepared for this complex process. Most likely, the procrastinating will continue.

Time is your best friend in the exit process, when creating a long term strategic financial plan and when training the next generation of management. Both of these processes can take years.

"I can probably do this myself."

You know how to run your business, but have you ever exited a business? Remember, what got you *here,* will not get you *there.*

As a business owner you have already had conversations with your accountant, lawyer, insurance agent, financial planner and many other professionals. The information is probably scattered, isolated and focused. In other words, your information is not comprehensive, cohesive or holistic.

An owner might be able to juggle advice from disparate advisors and successfully exit their business. However, the odds of success will improve with a comprehensive exit plan and with the guidance of an exit planning professional.

"My business is worth $10 million."

The reality is that most owners overvalue their business and have a false impression of its actual worth. Simply because an owner has spent 30 years working 60 hours per week does not necessarily mean that value has been created in a company. The actual value of a business is what someone is willing to pay for your business.

A business has different values depending on who is buying the business. This is called a "range of values." An owner should base the value of their business on the exit strategy they are trying to employ. And the owner should learn what makes your business more valuable to an acquiring party.

Advisors accredited in business appraisals are trained in these situations and should be engaged to provide you with the guidance of increasing business value.

"That will never happen to me."

Death, divorce, disease, disability. Many business owners fail to plan for unexpected hardships. Those who do prepare are protecting their business for the long term.

Beacon Exit Planning gets a call once a month regarding an owner's untimely death or disability. In most cases, the buy-sell agreements are not aligned with the business owner's motives or goals. Often, they are unfunded or established in a manner that creates more ambiguity than clarity

One recent horror story left the owner in court several years, costing both parties hundreds of thousands of dollars in legal fees without a clear end in sight. In another case, an owner's widow, who never worked in the business, was demanding her husband's office, position and salary. We worked with another company with an existing buy-sell agreement that, in the event of the owner's death, would unintentionally create income tax liability for the owner's widow.

These situations are examples of the unintended consequences that result from an outdated or poorly drafted cookie cutter agreement contingency plan. Creating or updating contingency plan documents, such as buy-sell agreements, will be a key step in building a successful exit plan.

"If I could get $8 million, I would retire tomorrow."

Owners often underestimate the amount of money they will need after they leave a business. The real question you should be asking is: How much do I need to replace my income and not outlive my money?

An owner must consider their money outside the business, including your savings, retirement funds, real estate income, investments, etc. From there, he or she can develop an estimate of the amount needed to replace their income in the long term.

"My accountant does exit planning."

You probably have a good accountant. And you might have an estimate of the value of your company. But it takes a proactive approach and coordinating of ideas and documents to exit a business. What your exiting advisors don't know about the exiting process might cost you millions.

Exit planners can navigate this process and get you the most out of your exit. Exit planners are trained as process consultants to move an owner on a path that will meet his or her goals and end financial target—to replace the owner and to protect their wealth with a comprehensive holistic result.

Once an owner understands the common misconceptions of exiting, he or she can begin to develop the plan itself. The plan will focus on three areas—business, personal and financial planning.

Three Main Areas of Focus

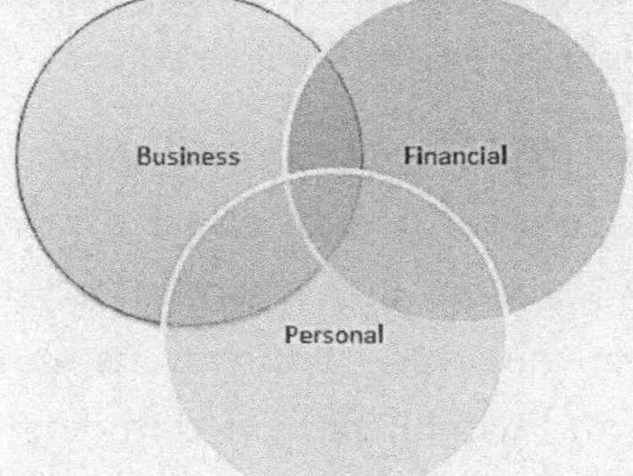

Who is coordinating the circles to help you meet your exiting goals?

Business planning

Business planning should consider many of the aspects of getting the business ready for a sale transaction. The following are tasks to consider:

Business valuation. Understanding the value of your company is paramount to alleviating any unrealistic expectations that a business owner might foster. Every owner should have their business appraised and work with the appraiser to better understand what creates value and what detracts value in their business. This will help keep expectations in line with reality.

Succession planning. As mentioned in Chapter 1, it will become critical for the owner to train and grow a management team that can take the reins of the business once the owner has left the business. This is true whether the owner is selling to an outside buyer or through an internal transaction to employees or family.

Tax planning. Understanding the exposure and tax ramifications of a business exit will be critical in achieving financial goals. With some transactions incurring more than a 50 percent effective tax rate, it becomes more important to understand these consequences and to understand the available alternatives that can reduce your financial risk and obligation.

Transfer options. Each transfer option will have varying degrees of nuances that can have a substantial effect on the outcome for the business owner. Valuation and taxation vary most prominently between the types of transfers. The various transfer options were noted in Chapter 1 and will be explained in detail in Chapter 3.

Payment. The company will pay for everything during the exit transaction. The company becomes the proverbial goose that lays the golden egg. If a company doesn't perform well, the owner won't get paid. Therefore, it becomes even more important to protect and support the company during the exit. This concept holds true for internal and external exits. In an external exit the buyer is counting on the future company profits for a multi-year pay back.

In addition, an owner should implement sound asset protection techniques that will help minimize predatory litigation and lawsuits.

Personal planning

Personal planning, as the term suggests, encompasses the more personal aspects of running a business, including the owner's emotional attachment to the company, the owner's legacy goals and the owner's family relationships.

Emotional ties to the business. There is no question that exiting a business will have an emotional effect on a business owner. An owner who has been associated with their business for 20, 30 or even 40 or more years will undoubtedly have an emotional response, whether positive or negative, when preparing for their exit.

The owner must consider this and incorporate it into the planning process.

Legacy. Legacy addresses how the owner's exit will affect everyone who depends on the business and the company culture—the owner and their family members, the employees and their families, and potentially the community. Legacy issues are real and run deep into numerous lives. It is incumbent on the business owner to determine what his or her legacy will be and to what extent it will become a deciding factor in the exit strategy selected.

Family members in the business. Having family member in the business can create an additional layer of drama in the exiting process. A key issue that often arises is the adequacy of the family member's talent over, say, a key manager. Another such factor is entitlement syndrome, where the family member may feel entitled to certain rights and benefits that have not been earned. Do not kick the can down the road.

The business owner should confront any of these potential issues head on so as not to create a negative environment in the business and perhaps, just as importantly, maintain harmony at the Thanksgiving Day table.

Financial planning

The financial planning piece of exit planning establishes the steps an owner must take to achieve the financial goals for their exit. Some specifics considerations of financial planning:

Retirement planning. Without question the biggest reason for business owners postponing their exit planning process is the recognition that they don't know how much money they will need in retirement. The uncertainty is compounded by the fact that most of their wealth is *trapped* inside of their illiquid business.

We are living longer as a society and costs, particularly health care costs, continue to skyrocket. A business owner must learn and understand what income needs they will have in post-exit life. Once the owner can visualize their financial future, the process of exiting and succession can become clearer and more definitive.

Planning for family members. The process of transitioning a construction company will usually occur over time. A business owner should employ tactics to protect their family in the event of catastrophic occurrences such as death and disability. Life insurance, disability insurance, asset protection and comprehensive estate planning should always be considered so as not to create additional undue hardships to the family and company beyond the untimely event that just occurred.

Tax planning. Taxes top considerations in financial planning just as they do in business planning. The lack of planning for corporate, income, capital gain and estate taxes can significantly erode the owner's estate. An exit plan must consider these taxes and plan for the minimization of this burden to the family.

The next three chapters of this book are dedicated to exploring the three types of planning—business, personal and financial —in more depth.

Discovery, Analysis and Design

Once an owner has considered all of the elements that go into each type of planning, they are ready to begin creating the exit plan itself. The process can take from six to nine months to complete. This section presents Beacon Exit Planning's three-phase process for developing an exit plan that addresses the primary considerations of each area.

Exit planning is the orchestration and coordination of the various disciplines involved in an exit coordinated in one comprehensive report. That report defines all the options to determine the best fit for the owner's goals and navigates a path out of the business.

This combined information will give the owner the best overall result once the exit is complete. Beacon Exit Planning uses a proprietary process called **DAD**, which stands for Discovery,

Analysis and Design.

Discovery. During the first part of the exit planning process, Beacon Exit Planning interviews the business owner and spouse. The purpose is to identify the owner's goals and provide him or her with the opportunity to envision life outside the business. How does the owner envision the future ownership of the business to look? How does the owner envision life outside the business for themselves?

This process will provide the planner an opportunity to gain further insight into the world and life of the owner and his family. This portion of the process will serve as a guide for the rest of the planning exercise.

Analysis. During the analysis process, the planner will examine the in-place personal and corporate legal and financial documents, such as wills, trusts, buy/sell agreements, compensation agreements and life insurance policies. The key is to determine whether these documents support the goals that were identified in the Discovery phase.

In almost all cases, modifications are warranted because of outdated documents or because the cookie cutter strategies are not sufficient to alleviate the ambiguity that might arise if the documents were needed to be executed.

Design. The end product in an exit planning engagement is a comprehensive, fully customized report, or blue print, that outlines the goals established by the owner and illustrations and solutions for the owner to consider and implement.

Upon delivery we spend most of the day with the owner reviewing the plan. *This is not the end, but the beginning* of the process. The learning and coaching can take from six months, and in some cases over three years, to unfold into the final blueprint.

After the exit plan is finalized, the owner moves to the next stage, the *execution phase.* During this phase, an exit planner can be the voice of the owner to quarterback and coordinate the different disciplines and professional advisers, including attorneys, accountants, estate planners, insurance advisers, financial planners, business consultants and others involved the process.

BONUS ARTICLE

A Successful Exit

In running your business there is only one guarantee: you eventually will exit—either voluntarily or involuntarily. The day will come when you will have to say goodbye. Exiting is not an easy process, and the odds are not in your favor. To succeed, the business and the owner must both be prepared to successfully transfer the business.

This article will address the common confusion found in differentiating a business exit from a business succession. Both are needed to successfully exit your business, unlock your trapped wealth, protect your legacy and successfully move your company into the next generation or to an external buyer.

My experience has reaffirmed that a business owner cannot commit to the difficult emotional succession process (replacing themselves) until they can clearly envision their financial future (exit plan and retirement) and accept the reality that they will not outlive their money.

Link: http://beaconexitplanning.com/bookbonuses/

Notes

Chapter 3: Business Planning

"The next best thing to being wise oneself is to live in a circle of those who are." —C.S. Lewis

This chapter focuses on the business planning aspect of exit planning transfer options, business valuation and appraisals. Taxes are also a critical aspect of business planning. They are addressed briefly in this chapter and covered in-depth in Chapter 6: The Cost of Exiting.

We start with the transfer options available to business owners. As you begin to study the alternatives available, it is important to understand the nuances of the different strategies and the pros and cons that each brings to your overall exit strategy.

Transfer options

Owners have several options when it comes to transferring their business, from selling to an outside buyer to a management buyout. Each transfer method presents the owner with compromises and various questions of tax liability, business value, succession and more.

All exit vehicles can essentially be categorized as either internal and external.

Internal transfers are transfers within the organization, usually to family members, employees or key executives within the organization. These methods range from employee stock ownership plans (ESOPs), management buyouts (MBOs), selling to trusts and gifting.

These types of transfers can provide the seller with greater flexibility, control and favorable strategies to reduce financial risk. He or she can sell all or a portion of the business interest, maintain voting control and continue to receive salary and benefits. In addition, if properly structured, these methods can provide the greatest tax efficiencies.

The majority of internal transfers are structured as stock or equity sales, meaning that the seller will sell his stock or equity interests. These will be realized as capital gain transactions and be subjected to a lower transaction tax.

Management buyout. This is the most common method of transfer for contractor owners. Because of the inherent nature of construction companies, there is often too much risk associated with it for an outside buyer to purchase. Unless the construction company has developed a unique cash flow and not created a primarily project-based operations, selling to an outside party does not typically occur.

The buyers who typically see the best returns are those key executives working within the business. They understand the relationships, systems and operations. Because of the intimate knowledge with the business they are in a better position to manage the risk associated with transferring the business.

Management buyouts also create the greatest flexibility to a selling owner. He or she can sell a portion of the company today, take some chips off the table and continue to earn a salary and benefits. The owner can sell the rest of the company in the future or sell the entire company immediately. Because of this flexibility, a business owner can achieve great tax efficiency with the transaction.

A common, yet counterintuitive strategy, in a management buyout is to reduce the sales price of the company. A lower sales price will require less pre-tax income to be generated by the company and ultimately will lead to lower taxes.

Employee Stock Ownership Plan. The ESOP is probably the most tax efficient transaction that a seller can employ. It is the only transition method that can be monetized with pre-tax dollars. It does, however, come with its own nuances.

The ESOP, in all respects, is nothing more than another retirement plan. In its most simplistic terms an ESOP is similar to a profit-sharing plan where employees will vest in values associated with assets within the retirement plan trust. When funds are received within the trust, assets are purchased. The values of those assets are assigned to participant accounts based on factors such as years of service.

The big difference between an ESOP and a traditional retirement plan is that in a traditional profit sharing plan the trust acquires marketable securities such as stocks and mutual funds. With an ESOP the trust will acquire non-marketable securities—in this case the seller's, or exiting owner's, stock.

An ESOP comes with some expensive administrative costs and burdens. An owner should carefully consider costs and management requirements to make sure it is the appropriate transition method.

Gifting. Gifting, as implied in the name, involves gifting stock to new ownership. It is not a monetizing method of transfer. Rather, it is a tax- efficient way to transfer wealth to a second generation or trust through the utilization of valuation discounts.

Valuation discounts are applied in instances where the interest being sold is either non-marketable, meaning you can't covert it to cash in three days or less like you can with publicly traded stock, or non-controlling, meaning that a minority interest holder cannot effectuate change in an organization.

Because the minority interest holder cannot expect to receive any benefit from the investment until it is sold, then that interest would normally sell for a discounted value. Application of these discounts can substantially reduce the pro-rata value of the underlying stock or equity being transferred and as such becomes a great wealth transfer tool.

Of note, gifting is not a typical transition option for an exiting owner who will be dependent on the sale of the business to maintain their post-exit lifestyle. However, by gifting non-voting stock, a business owner can maintain control of the organization and continue to receive a salary and benefits until the control is passed on to the recipient of the stock.

External transfers are sales to buyers outside of the organization. These buyers might be competitors, strategic buyers or investment-minded buyers such as private equity groups looking to invest in the company, grow the value and then sell in the future for a greater value.

In these situations, the seller can typically receive a higher sales price. However, because of the structure, it can create a greater tax burden and realization of an overall lower amount of eventual cash harvest.

External sales present additional considerations for owners. For example, external transfers are typically structured as asset sales, meaning an external buyer will buy the assets of the business but reject the assumption of liabilities unless specifically stated.

Often, the buyer is not privy to the operations and history of the company. Undisclosed liabilities can rear their ugly head in the future, and this creates an increased level of risk for the buyer. Asset sales protect the buyer from these potential liabilities.

Before the liquidation, however, the business organization will have to pay off its existing liabilities. Therefore, if a company is laden with debt the remaining liquidation funds can be nominal.

This dilemma creates an increased need for tax and cash flow planning before the transaction is complete.

The various asset classes that are sold will be taxed at various tax rates from ordinary income tax rates to capital gain tax rates. If the seller is a C corporation, the gain on assets will all be taxed at the corporate tax rate with a secondary capital gain tax upon liquidation of cash and remaining assets from the entity.

The buyer on the other hand enjoys the benefits of an asset sale. The assets are usually written up to fair market value, which the buyer can now depreciate, usually in an accelerated method. This allows the buyer to recapture a portion of the purchase price through the depreciation deduction and eventual tax savings. There are no liabilities assumed by the buyer unless specifically enumerated in the final purchase and sale agreement.

Some specific notes about the two primary types of external transfers:

Sale to outside party. Outside parties refer to individuals or entities looking to gain market share or see complementary services or products that will enhance their existing product or service. This type of sale can provide greater returns for the seller, if the buyer sees a substantial opportunity to grow their existing line of business.

Some outside, strategic buyers make acquisitions in order to purchase market share. In these situations, the buyer will often pay the tangible net asset value with only a small amount of goodwill.

Sale to a private equity group. Private equity sales are typically investment related. The private equity firm will acquire a controlling interest in the business and recapitalize it with financial and human capital in an effort to substantially grow the business and sell it at an increased profit some several years down the road.

For the seller, private equity sales provide an opportunity to get a second bite of the apple. By this, we mean the owner will sell a controlling interest at the outset, then sell the minority interest in the shares at some future point in time when the value of the business has been increased.

Asset protection

Understanding the fundamental pros and cons to the various exit strategies is critical for the business owner. However, as an owner gets closer to exiting, one principal investment fundamentals should come the forefront: preservation of capital.

Owners must consider methods of protecting the business and the business' assets. As mentioned previously, the business is considered the goose that lays the golden egg in the owner's exit, meaning the company will pay for everything including salaries, benefits and the eventual sales proceeds to the seller. In other words, the success of an owner's exit depends on the success of the company and the protection of the business' assets.

With so much at stake, it is critical for the business owner to establish asset protection strategies. Asset protection is essentially the careful structuring of the business operations in a manner that provides limited opportunities for creditors and predatory lawsuits to access assets of the business.

Understanding the difference between the entity types and the protection that they bring is critical. Most owners do not realize that because they are a corporation their assets can still be attached in the event of a judgement against the company.

Most business owners who own the real estate that the business operates are already utilizing asset protection strategies. They typically establish the business in one entity with limited liability characteristics and then establish another entity, usually a limited liability company to hold the real estate.

In a more comprehensive structure, the operating business can be further segregated into additional entities, such as a management company and a leasing company. This process isolates the assets from both entities. It prevents them from being commingled and limits the potential exposure to predatory lawsuits.

Owners should also consider domicile where the company will be established. Certain states are more business friendly and provide greater protection for sellers in exposing assets to lawsuits.

Business valuation

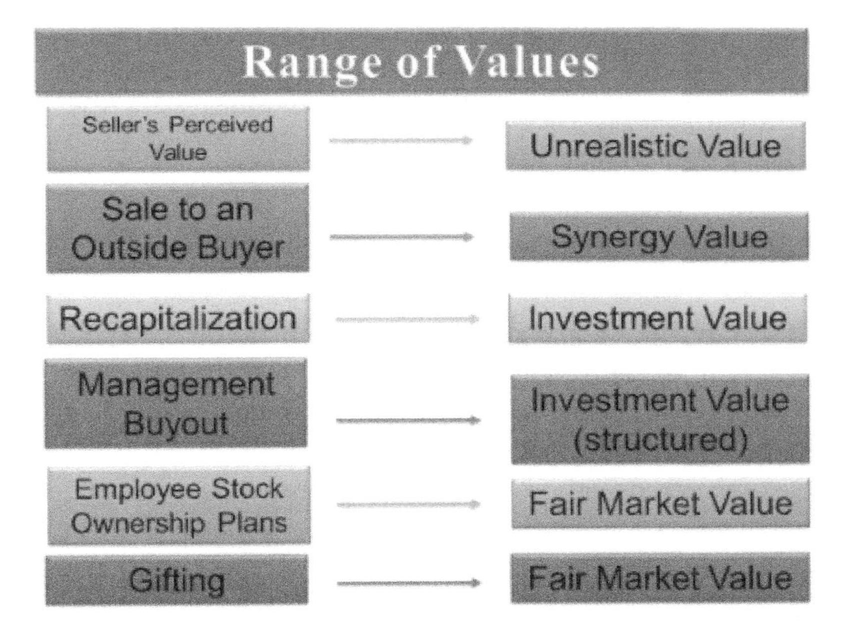

As discussed in Chapter 2, valuation is a complicated, yet critical, consideration in a business exit. During the planning stage, a business appraiser should be consulted to best determine a company's value but to also consider and understand what adds value and what is detracting value from the business.

Part of what makes business valuation such a tricky task is that closely held businesses carry a range of values at any given point in time. The chosen exit option will be the single greatest determinant of the value. A business will be valued at one number for a gift or internal sale and can be valued at another for an external sale.

In simple terms, the value of a business is equal to its cash flow times a market multiple.

Cash flow. An appraiser might use a controlling interest cash flow stream, a minority interest cash flow stream or even a strategic buyer's cash flow stream. The quality of the chosen cash flow stream will play a significant role in determining the overall value.

A company's cash flow should not be dependent on a single customer or an individual within the organization. This creates a greater dependency on that customer or individual and thus creates risk. That overall risk is the component of market multiple.

Market multiple. A market multiple is simply the inverse of a rate of return that an investor would seek in return for investing in your business. Therefore, a cash flow stream that is dependent on certain individuals or customer would create a greater risk for a potential buyer and, as such, would demand a greater rate of return on his or her investment (and a lower multiple).

To put this concept into perspective, let's take a look at two construction companies: Alpha Company and Beta Company. Each company generates $10 million in revenue and both net $1 million in net profit.

Alpha Company's sole source of revenue is derived from contracts that were awarded through the lowest bidder process.

Conversely, Beta Company generates its revenue through a variety of sources. It has a service and maintenance department that generates substantial margins on its services. It also generates a substantial portion of its business from negotiated work, and an additional source of revenue is generated from bid work.

Based on these facts, Beta Company would demand a higher market multiple due to the diversified quality of cash flow. Alpha Company's cash flow is generated from bid work that is open to all other contractors in the industry and is in constant pressure for the lowest price. Meanwhile Beta Company generates a more diverse source of cash flow. Because of the maintenance contracts and relationships, it creates less transferability risk for the buyer.

As mentioned above, valuation requires more than just cash flow and market multiples. There are four basic standards of values that can be applied to the transfer of a business: net asset or book value, fair market value, fair value or financial value, and strategic value.

Net asset value/book value. The net asset value is considered the "floor" of the valuation spectrum. The net asset value considers the net tangible assets that can be sold in an orderly fashion, the liabilities paid and the net proceeds that would be recognized by the seller. This value should be used only as a benchmark for the other values.

Fair market value. Fair market value comes into play during ESOP and gifting transactions. The universal definition for fair market value in the appraisal world comes from an IRS Revenue Ruling 59-60 that defines the value of a company as, "The price at which the property would change hands between a willing buyer and a willing seller when the buyer is not under any compulsion to buy and the seller is not under any compulsion to sell, and both parties having reasonable knowledge of relevant facts. The hypothetical buyer and seller are assumed to be able and willing to trade and to be well informed about the property and concerning the market for such property." In other words, the value is based upon all of the information available to the parties at that point in time.

Fair value/financial value. Management buyouts or private equity transactions rely on fair value to determine a business' valuation. Fair or financial value refers to the company's value according to requirements and expectations set by a particular investor. It is the capitalized value of future cash flows at a desired rate of return.

Management buyout or private equity transactions are not required to use a specific formula as required in fair market value calculations. Each investor can bring in a different offer that is based on the potential buyers' expectations and perceptions about the inherent risk associated with the investment.

Strategic value. The final standard of value that could be utilized in determining the value of a closely held business is called strategic value, which can be equated to investment value. This standard of value is primarily used when a sale is made to an industry or strategic buyer.

When a company is sold to an industry buyer, there are economies of scale with certain expenses. These synergistic costs, or duplicate costs such as bookkeeping, administration, rent, will be eliminated in the calculation of the discretionary cash flow, thereby increasing the business value to a potential buyer.

BONUS TOOL

Beacon Online Valuation and Value Drivers

The odds of selling your business are not in your favor. Only 20 percent of businesses that actually go to market see the closing table. It is important to understand and invest in making your business saleable.

The following bonus tool is being offered to you so that you can identify areas of strength and weakness in your business and how it affects it overall value. It can mean the difference of getting three times and five times multiples for your business or selling altogether.

Upon completion of the survey you will be provided with:

1. A risk score that evaluates the strength or weakness of key value drivers
2. An estimate of value for your business

Link: http://bit.ly/beaconvaluation

Notes

Chapter 4: Personal Planning

As mentioned in Chapter 2, the key areas to focus on in the personal planning section of your exit plan are the emotional ties to the business, family members' involvement in the business and the legacy that you would like to leave behind once you have left the business.

For many business owners, their business is not what they do, but who they are. They have strong emotional attachments to their business and to their work within the business. The emotional attachment that is reflected in an owner's longtime dedicated business leadership can become a *major obstacle* when it comes time for the owner to exit their business.

Emotional attachment should be confronted at the front end of the planning process. Some specific considerations:

Don't procrastinate. Procrastination is a telltale sign that a business owner's emotional attachment is standing in the way of their exit planning. It is a sign that the owner is having difficulty letting go. The owner is *stuck* and either has no plan for an exit or has no intention of exiting.

Putting off exiting planning is a common among business owners. However, waiting until you are ready to exit your business before you start to get the business ready for transition lessens your probability of success. Time can be your best friend or your worst enemy.

Beacon Exit Planning recommends that owners begin to prepare for their eventual exit even if they aren't ready to leave immediately. There are numerous tasks—many of which can take years—that must be completed well in advance of the owner's actual departure.

Consider emotional attachment in transfer decisions. The type of emotional attachment an owner has with their business should be factored into their choice of transfer option.

For instance, when a business owner has a positive attachment to the business and a bond to protecting their company associates, selling to an outside party might not be the best fit as an exiting alternative. In this situation an internal exit such as an employee stock ownership plan (ESOP) or management buyout (MBO) may be the better alternative.

Conversely, consider a business owner who is burnt out, or an owner who is facing a medical or family condition that is forcing the exit. For these owners, the urgency of an outside sale would make the most sense.

Plan for family members who are in the business. The next issue that needs to be addressed in the personal planning sphere is family, especially family involved in the business. Many business owners have family members involved in the business at many levels.

Some will never become owners, because they do not want the burden or risk associated with the ownership or because they aren't capable of doing so. Then there are the family members who have risen to a professional level are demonstrating leadership that are destined to become eventual owners.

Each family situation in a business is unique, much like every exit is unique. Our experiences have shown that situations where the exiting family member has taken the time to formally train, hold accountable, educate and stretch the succeeding family member sees better results. The successor family member should learn the business from the bottom up, much like the exiting owner did. Essentially the successor owner must earn their leadership and respect from their team and associates.

The company employees understand that the natural progression into the next generation is a member of family. What they will not respect is the idea that a son or daughter of the exiting business owner starts from the top, doesn't respect other teammates, and feels that they have a right to ownership and the benefits that a business owner enjoys, without considering the associated risks that go along with business ownership.

If family dynamics become an issue and an obstacle for transition, there are numerous coaches in the marketplace who specialize in family dynamics and can assist with the process. This can be a useful exercise and one that could pay a substantial return on investment. The return can be more than monetary, which in some cases can be more valuable.

Set legacy goals. The final component of the personal planning sphere is the business owner's legacy. For many, the business has become the sole source of financial support. The business has supported a lifestyle for the owner, his or her family, the employees and in some cases the community.

Many owners have become pillars in the community, serving on various boards and providing charitable contributions to various organizations to help the community. If the owner is no longer with the company, how will the business and social community fare without them?

That is a question that the business owner must consider. For many owners, giving back to the community is an integral part of their lives. Many don't want to have to let 200 employees go and have them find jobs elsewhere.

For these owners the planning process takes on a more expanded role. They not only want to make sure the business is monetized, but they want to ensure that provisions are put in place to support other *legacy goals*.

To support future legacy goals, an owner should provide cultural direction to the successors on the importance of various legacy issues, and on the importance of keeping the business in operating form so that the future generations of owners and employees can enjoy the benefits that the business can provide them.

BONUS ARTICLE

Buy Sell Agreement Landmines

Over the past 20+ years, Beacon exit planners have met with hundreds of business owners around the country consulting on a variety of topics including tax, business valuation, exit planning and risk management. Owners spend virtually their entire lives building their businesses with the hopes of creating a valuable asset that they can eventually sell or transfer in order to achieve a lifetime of financial independence.

Anyone who has walked in those shoes can tell you that it's not as easy as it sounds. The journey from starting a business to the eventual monetization of this illiquid asset is plagued with landmines along the way. One such landmine that we encounter on a regular basis is an improperly created buy/sell agreement.

A buy/sell agreement is a document drafted between two or more business owners that addresses how an ownership interest is to be liquidated in the case of life events such as death, disability, divorce, departure (whether voluntary or involuntary) and dissolution. This document is meant to clarify and simplify the process during this difficult time in a business' life cycle.

Link: http://beaconexitplanning.com/bookbonuses/

Notes

Chapter 5: Financial Planning

The final stage of planning for a business transfer and exit addresses the owner's financial needs after he or she leaves the company. This stage of planning can be daunting, uncertain and emotionally charged.

As a business owner, you have always been in control of your personal and business finances. You have been able to make changes within the organization to control the company's cash flow and your income. When you leave the business, this will change. You will be on a fixed income, and that income will be required to cover all known and unknown costs throughout retirement. This can be intimidating, particularly when you consider the reality of longer life expectancies, health care costs that are spiraling out of control and an overall rising cost of living.

In your financial plan, you will determine the best strategy for monetizing your business in a way that will replace your income and allow you to maintain your lifestyle in the long term. You will likely only get one chance to do it right—to determine the after-tax payment that you need to get out of the business in a way that creates sufficient income.

Unfortunately, most owners have not saved enough for retirement to maintain their existing lifestyle. They have reinvested their excess profits and cash into growing their business. They have now created a valuable asset that is not only illiquid, but also houses the majority of the owner's wealth.

In our experience at Beacon Exit Planning, most business owners have 70 percent or more of their wealth trapped in their illiquid business. We worked with one owner for whom that number was as high as 92 percent. These owners are completely dependent on the monetizing of the business to be able to support their post exit lifestyle in retirement. If they don't, that wealth they have accumulated over decades will be lost.

This chapter will take an owner through the financial planning stage of a business exit. It presents the primary objectives of an owner's financial plan, offers a straightforward method of calculating future financial needs and looks at options for managing financial risks.

Financial plan objectives

A successful financial plan will answer a number of critical questions for an exiting owner. For example, how much money will I need in the long term? How much will I need from my business exit to ensure I don't run out of money in retirement? How can I protect my family in the event that something happens to me?

The objectives of a financial plan can be divided into two categories:

Envisioning a financial future. A thorough financial planning analysis allows the exiting business owner to envision their financial future after the harvest of their largest illiquid asset, the business. Only with this financial clarity can the owner determine whether he or she can afford to retire comfortably and not outlive their money, or whether they will need to make lifestyle changes post-exit.

Managing risk. The financial plan will help an owner implement risk management techniques that will protect the owner, the business and the owner's family. As an owner of a construction company, you are no stranger to risk. Personal assets can be exposed to predatory and frivolous lawsuits much like your business assets. Risk management will consider potential tax consequences, both of the sale and future estate taxes. Surprise tax liabilities can become a major financial burden to an owner or to their family.

Risk management also addresses how the business and family will be protected if something catastrophic happens to the owner. Events such as death and disability could derail the financial future of the owner and their family, particularly for families that are deeply dependent on the business income.

Asset calculations

Once an owner envisions their financial future, they will be able to calculate how much wealth they will need to cover their future long-term costs. That number should then be subtracted from the owner's current liquid assets combined with estimates of other sources of income. The resulting figure is what the owner will need to harvest from the business transaction, after taxes. In other words:

What you have

\- What you need

Required Proceeds from Business Sale

(Net of tax)

If the result of this equation is a positive number, then the owner has sufficiently saved enough liquid assets to support his post-exit lifestyle. The focus should then be centered on the strategies for monetizing that wealth and managing the taxation effect of the transaction.

If the result of the calculation is a negative number, the business owner will be dependent on the value of the business for maintaining his or her lifestyle. In cases where the owner is relying on the sale to support themselves in the future, financial planning should focus on valuation and net-after-tax results. This will allow an owner to determine if there will be sufficient net proceeds to support that deficiency.

It is no surprise that most business owners fit in the latter part of this scenario. As previously mentioned, owners reinvest profits and cash to build a significant asset that now needs to be monetized in order to realize that value.

If the transaction cannot support the deficiency, then the owner needs to consider other avenues such as increasing the value of the business, changing lifestyle or staying in the business for a longer time and beginning a more aggressive savings program.

Financial strategies

There is a fundamental concept in financial planning that suggests that the closer an investor is to needing the invested capital, the more conservative the risk tolerance and investment strategy. There is also a concept that suggests that diversification can help mitigate any concentration in one particular type of security.

These recommendations can be difficult for business owners to meet. A business owner with 70-to-80 percent of wealth in a closely held business can neither diversify their portfolio until the asset is sold, nor can he or she change their investment strategy to substantiate a more conservative risk tolerance. So, what is an owner to do?

First the financial planning should be coordinated with the owner's business planning process. For example, contingency planning. In the event of a death or disability, the personal financial plan should consider what provisions, if any, are being made to compensate the departing business owner and their family. That compensation should then be compared to the owner's financial needs. If there is not enough to support the family, then the owner should consider purchasing life insurance to help fill the gap.

Life insurance. Life insurance is a fantastic tool. It can provide a substantial tax-free benefit in a rather difficult situation, and it can help provide for the payment of stock acquisition and estate taxes.

In a recent case, Beacon Exit Planning worked with a family reviewing their estate planning needs and potential tax obligations in the event of the business owner's demise. This was a successful family that had done a great job building their business and diversifying with real estate and other liquid assets. After all the hard work they had put into building the portfolio of assets, the result was a potential estate tax obligation of $4 million.

We determined that rather than cutting a check for $4 million to the government upon the owner's death, the estate could save approximately $3.5 million in cash by acquiring a life insurance policy that would cover the owner's life expectancy for about 10 percent of the tax obligation.

Asset protection. Another strategy that should be employed by the business owner and his or her family is asset protection of personal and business assets. An owner's personal assets are often left unprotected. The owner and their advisors assume that the majority of risk is derived from the business, and as a result, asset protection strategies are only applied to business assets.

However, that is simply not the case. In this litigious world that we live in, lawsuits can come in many forms. An individual can be sued for an action where he or she was not even involved, exposing all personal assets to predatory lawsuits.

An owner can protect their personal assets through a number of means, including titling personal asset in the name of entities with protective characteristics such as trust, limited liability companies or limited partnerships. These entities by their inherent nature provide protection from outside creditors, making it difficult for attachment by a creditor.

For business owners these are a few strategies that should be considered in financial planning. They will provide safety nets to the owners and their families in the event of a catastrophic event.

Notes

Chapter 6: The Cost of Exiting

One of the most critical obstacles you will face in your business exit is the actual cost of transitioning your company to new ownership. Over the years, you have spent countless hours monitoring the business costs in order to run a profitable business. Now, you are facing the final transaction of your ownership career, and you need to make sure you—and your company—aren't swallowed by the costs of exiting.

As an exiting owner, you will confront costs from several directions during the exit process. These include taxes, fees and the very real potential cost of not getting paid.

One way to increase the probability of success is to make a plan and incorporate these costs and risks within your plan. A plan will allow you to advance your thinking about each type of exit strategy while getting a better understanding of the associated values and costs related with your exiting strategies.

Taxes

Three parties involved in every deal: the buyer, the seller and Uncle Sam. Uncle Sam's only purpose in the transaction is to collect as much of your harvest as you're willing to give him.

The tax ramifications to exiting a business can be substantial. Under the wrong circumstances an owner can pay out in excess of 50 percent of the entire sales price. On the other hand, tax rates can be as low as zero if the proper conditions exist. Exiting owners must design an exit strategy that minimizes the overall tax yield on the transaction.

There are several key factors that play a role on the amount of taxes an owner will pay upon the sale of the business, including the exit method, the company's legal formation, the deal structure and the advisor's knowledge in exit strategy taxation.

But first, an owner should understand a few key tax terms and treatments that will likely arise during their exit:

Tax exemption. The elimination of taxation on the transaction such as the tax benefits available to an owner selling to an employee stock ownership plan.

Tax deferral. The deferral of taxation until a time when it will be more cost effective due to the seller's reduced income level in retirement and as such will be subjected to a lower overall tax rate.

Capital gains treatment. The preferred tax rates associated with selling business assets or equity.

Ordinary income tax treatment, without payroll taxes. A transaction taxed at graduated tax rates ranging from 0 percent to 37 percent.

Ordinary income tax treatment, with payroll taxes. Transactions taxed at graduated income tax rates ranging from 0 percent to 37 percent, with the addition of social security and Medicare taxes at a combined rate of 15.3 percent. In 2013, the Patient Protection and Affordable Care Act implemented an additional 3.8 percent Medicare tax on all investment income and a .9 percent on earned income in excess of $250,000.

Small Business Income Deduction. In December 2017, Congress passed the Tax Cut and Jobs Act. Among other provisions the act provided for an exclusion from taxable income up to 20 percent for certain qualified business income. The full exclusion would create an effective tax rate on business income of approximately 29.6 percent for pass through entities such as partnerships, S corporation and Limited Liability Companies. C corporations have experienced the greatest reduction of taxes with the rates dropping to 21 percent on taxable income.

Exit type

The exit method will be a significant contributor to the amount of taxes that will need to be paid. In every exit method except the employee stock ownership plan, the transaction will be paid with after-tax dollars. This means that the higher the sales price of the deal, the more income tax that needs to be paid to net the desired sale price.

More specific details about the tax penalties of the various transaction vehicles are presented in Chapter 3.

Corporate structure

Another factor to consider when planning for taxes during the exit is the taxable entity formation of the company. Most companies are structured as either C corporations, S corporations, Limited Liability Companies (LLCs), partnerships or sole proprietorships.

C corporations are more heavily taxed than many other types of entities, primarily because they are subject to double taxation. Additionally, C corporations are not eligible for capital gains tax rates but are subject to built-in gains tax upon S conversion. However, the C corporation allows an owner to offset various tax obligations by utilizing net operating losses from prior years, if they are available. These entities generally are most tax inefficient if the assets, rather than the stock, are sold.

Of note, the Tax Cut and Jobs Act that signed into law in December 2017 reduced the C corporate tax rate to a flat 21 percent. This is a significant reduction from the prior graduated rates, with the highest bracket at 39 percent. While this is attractive from an annual income tax basis, there will still be a second layer of taxation when the company distributes income from the corporation.

LLCs and S corporations, on the other hand, receive more favorable tax treatment. They are subject to only a single layer of taxation whereby gains, losses, income and deductions flowing through to the individual members/shareholders are taxed at their respective individual tax rates. Owners of C corporations can consider restructuring their company as an S corporation to reduce their tax penalty.

Partnerships and sole proprietors are considered disregarded entities, meaning the IRS does not recognize them as an individual taxed entity. All assets are treated as though they are owned by the individual owners and taxes accordingly.

Deal structure

The final point that needs to be made regarding the effect on taxes to be paid on the sale of the business is the deal structure. There are generally two methods for transferring the business: asset sale and stock sale.

Asset sale. The asset sale, as discussed in Chapter 3, is often used in the transfer of a business between the company and an outside party. The asset sale provides greater advantages to the buyer.

Outside sales are generally structured as asset sales, allowing the buyer to avoid the known and unknown liabilities of the purchased company. Additionally, asset sales allow the buyer to recover a portion of the purchase price through depreciation.

Stock sale. The stock sale provides greater advantages to the seller. In a stock sale transaction, the buyer essentially steps into the shoes of the seller, assuming the assets and the liabilities, both known and unknown.

A stock sale is significantly less complicated than an asset sale.

The buyer purchases the shares at the established price, and it becomes the basis or cost in the investment. The seller, on the other hand, recognizes capital gain between the sales price and the cost basis in the investment and is taxed at the more favorable capital gains rates.

We'll close this section on taxes with an example from our work at Beacon Exit Planning, to demonstrate how careful consideration of taxes during exit planning can make a real difference.

Several years ago, we worked with a client who operated several C corporation entities and wanted to begin the exit planning process. The client was concerned about the 50 or more percent tax obligation that was staring him in the face. We were concerned that the owner had to sell 13 separate corporations and incur the onerous tax obligations of C corporation for each of the 13.

After careful consideration, we developed a strategy to consolidate several of the client's entities under a newly created holding company. We then converted them to S corporations and made the necessary elections with the IRS. This was a tax-free reorganization.

Additionally, the reorganization created a more efficient organization. The mere efficiencies in purchasing power created an increase in gross profit and, when plugged into the valuation model several million dollars of value was created.

Most owners would be thrilled that an organizational restructuring created several million dollars in value. Our client, however, was a savvy business owner and recognized that the increased value in turn created a larger tax obligation to him because the amount of net proceeds required to pay the sales price mandated more profits and, therefore, more in taxes.

This problem was easily solved by reducing the value of the underlying stock sale, reallocating resources to more tax efficient tools and establishing a strategy that completely eliminated the capital gains tax. The result was a savings of several million dollars in taxes and a business owner with substantially more dollars in the bank.

Fees

The second category of costs that an owner is confronted with in a business exit comes from advisory fees—the fees charged by the team of advisors necessary in a business exit.

Beyond the traditional CPA and attorney fees, an owner may also incur costs from other specialist advisors, such as investment bankers, ESOP specialists, estate planning attorneys, etc. Fees are an inevitable conclusion in the process. Exit planning is a multi-disciplined endeavor and, as such, will require the skills and talents of various advisors.

Fee structures will vary based on the advisor who participates in the process. Beacon Exit Planning tends to utilize a flat fee in our planning process with an hourly component to the execution. Most advisors will bill on an hourly basis while others, such as investment bankers and brokers, tend to get paid as a commission or success fee.

Each one of the advisors plays a very important role in the process. However, it's important to understand that advisors don't get paid unless they perform a service. Sellers should make certain that the advisor supports the overall goals of the seller and is working in coordination with the plan.

One final note about fees. All too often, we see business owners chasing advisors. They hear about certain exit strategies such as management buyouts or ESOPs and chase advisors for answers. The result is sporadic, non-comprehensive information with each advisor promoting their service.

To better ensure the chance of success, the business owner should consider making an investment with an independent exit planner. The exit planner will provide no other service but comprehensive planning.

Here you can be assured that the plan and strategies provided will be in the owner's best interest and not the advisors'. Once the planning process has been completed and each strategy alternative is properly vetted the execution can be much more efficient and ultimately less costly.

Financial risk

The final cost associated with exiting a business is, simply, the cost of not getting paid. Beacon Exit Planning classifies this as financial risk, or the risk of not getting paid.

Financial risk is a particularly important consideration in management buyouts but can be prevalent in any situation where the owner doesn't receive all cash at closing. In an MBO, the proceeds to purchase the owner's shares will be derived from the profits of the business operations. Therefore, receiving the total sales price for the shares will be dependent on the future profitability and success of the business operations.

If the owner sells fractional ownership interests, he or she may continue to control the operations as long as they maintain a controlling interest in voting stock. Should the owner sell a sufficient number of voting shares to relinquish control of the company, the exiting owner will place the success of their exit into the hands of the management team. This may or may not be a problem depending on the skills of the succeeding management team.

Financial risk is not exclusive to the MBO. Any owner who sells his business in exchange for some future payment is subject to financial risk. Typical structures in other areas of business transition include seller financing and earn outs.

Seller financing means the seller will finance a portion of the transaction. In these transactions, it is imperative that the seller have a collateral interest in the stock. Should there be a default in payments, the seller will have the ability to retake the business.

There are two problems of note with seller financing, and both come with a high risk of non-payment. First, if payments aren't being made, there is a high probability that the company is in poor financial condition. Second, if the payments stop several years into an owner's retirement, how motivated will the owner be to come back and begin rebuilding the business?

An earn out provision, on the other hand, requires that the company meet certain financial benchmarks before the seller can receive the balance of his sales proceeds. The seller should negotiate for some operational control over the production process and have a good understanding of the formula for collection, including allocation of overhead expenses which can be used to "load" the income statement. Loading the income statement can artificially reduce the profitability, which causes the seller to miss his financial benchmarks as established, thus not get paid the balance of the sales price.

Each of these methods for recovering the sales prices are contingent upon the success and future profitability of the company. Adding to the risk is that the seller often must give up voting control of the entity and is at the mercy of the buyer.

Careful consideration should be given when structuring a deal that calls for future payments, particularly an earn out where the recovery of the sales price is contingent upon the business achieving certain financial benchmarks. This strategy leaves room for much manipulation and presents the potential for the seller to never receive the balance of that sales price.

There are ways that a business owner can mitigate financial risk. The best protection is to maintain voting control over the corporate stock. This provides the selling owner the opportunity to make final financial and operational decisions that may have a material adverse effect on the business.

Adding up the costs of exiting

We will close out this chapter with examples of how the costs might add up in various types of exits. The following table depicts financial scenarios that a business owner could expect on a $10 million transaction that is paid out over 10 years.

The illustration is based on a specific set of facts and circumstances. It is in no way intended to depict all exiting owner situations. The purpose of the chart is to provide you with an understanding of the significant tax and fee differences that could exist by using alternative strategies for the same business entity. Each transaction is unique and should be thoroughly analyzed to reflect the best possible outcome for your situation.

Furthermore, the following illustration depicts a stock sale. Should a business owner enter into an asset sale the structure of the transaction has many variables such as sales price allocation, asset basis, and unpaid balance sheet obligations, to name a few. Each of these characteristics that are present will have a significant effect on the net proceeds to the seller.

Lastly the type of entity structure will also have a substantial effect on taxation. This chart illustrates an S corporation with a specific set of facts and circumstances. C corporation transactions will have a substantially different outcome. Detailed descriptions of the previously discussed relevant tax treatments are outlined below the table for reference.

These computations must be a critical part of your exit plan.

	Payroll Bonus	ESOP**	Stock Redemption	TPT*** Plan
Sales Price (Stress on Company)	$ 15,519,640	$ 10,000,000	$ 14,204,545	$ 14,204,545
Taxes paid	(5,519,640)	-	(4,204,545)	(4,204,545)
Fees paid	(20,000)	(75,000)	(20,000)	(25,000)
Proceeds to seller (ESOP FMV)	9,980,000	9,925,000	9,980,000	9,975,000
Basis in Stock	(1,250,000)	(1,250,000)	(1,250,000)	(1,250,000)
Capital gain on sale of stock	8,730,000	8,675,000	8,730,000	8,725,000
Cap gains paid by seller - 23.8%***	(2,077,740)	(2,064,650)	(2,077,740)	-
Net Proceeds to Sellers	**$ 7,902,260**	**$ 7,860,350**	**$ 7,902,260**	**$ 9,975,000**
Recap				
Paid	$ 15,519,640	$ 10,000,000	$ 14,204,545	$ 14,204,545
Total Taxes and Fees Paid	$ 7,617,380	$ 2,139,650	$ 6,302,285	$ 4,229,545
Net	**$ 7,902,260**	**$ 7,860,350**	**$ 7,902,260**	**$ 9,975,000**
Effective Rate of Proceed Erosion	**49.08%**	**21.40%**	**44.37%**	**29.78%**

*** Utilizing 1042 rollover - no taxes to seller*

**** Utilizing Corporate Distribution codes sections eliminated Cap Gain*

Tax treatments common in exits

- **Tax exemption.** To eliminate the taxation on the transaction.
- **Tax deferral.** To defer taxation to a time where it is more cost effective.
- **Capital gains treatment.** The preferred tax rates associated with selling business assets or equity. Rates are at 0 percent, 10 percent or 20 percent depending on your income level. The Net Investment Income Tax of 3.8 percent will also be added once income levels reach $250,000.
- **Ordinary income tax treatment without payroll taxes.** Transactions taxed at graduated tax rates ranging from 0 percent to 37 percent.
- **Ordinary income tax treatment with payroll taxes.** Transactions taxed at graduated income tax rates ranging from 0 percent to 37 percent with the addition of social security and Medicare taxes at a combined rate of 15.3 percent. In 2013, the Patient Protection and Affordable Care Act implemented an additional 3.8 percent Medicare tax on all investment income and a .9 percent on earned income in excess of $250,000.
- **Tax on pass-through corporate income.** In 2017, Congress passed the 2017 Tax Cut and Jobs Act that essentially expands the income brackets, lowers the income tax rates and creates a new business deduction equal to 20 percent of business income. The deduction is subject to limitations; however, the net effective tax rate for business income will be 29.6 percent versus the highest individual income tax rate of 37 percent.

- **Tax on C corporation income.** The act reduces the C corporation tax rate to 21 percent from the previous 35 percent.

Notes

Chapter 7: Succession Planning

Succession replaces the owner by moving the chosen performers into a championship team, then into leadership and a process to replace the CEO/owner. This requires time, training and stretching of the team members.

An entire book could be written on succession. This chapter will provide an overview.

Successful succession is one critical aspect of an exit. If you cannot replace yourself, you will be stuck in your business without a buyer.

To succeed in this challenging succession process, *both the company and the owner* must be ready for a successful transition. It is critical that the management team and future CEO are ready to move into their new roles, so the present owner can, over time, relinquish the day-to-day management, leadership and strategic role in the business.

To achieve this, the company needs a strategic succession plan. As opposed to an exit plan, a succession plan provides a customized written map that focuses on the human side of a business, versus a financial side of the process.

A flexible plan may take several months to write and several years to execute. Depending on the readiness of a company's management and the type of exit and current payout, a succession plan may last from three to 10 years.

On the other hand, if the business is systematized and has strong financials with mature management in place and the owner can take a four-week vacation, then the company could be sale ready in less than two years.

To help guide owners through their succession process, Beacon Exit Planning developed a list of steps owners should follow to improve their succession process.

Complete your exit plan.

The succession process does not begin until an owner can begin to see himself or herself outside the business. The owner must visualize their financial future and set a conceptual retirement date. This occurs during exit planning.

Having an exit plan in place allows an owner to envision himself or herself as financially independent of the business. This liberates the owner, so they can plan for retirement and succession.

Establish a clear direction and focus.

The beginning of the succession process is a time for the senior management team to revisit the strategic plan, vision and mission. This process will be an exercise for the management team members to establish their roles, work as a team and grow their stake in the company's future.

It will be the management team's responsibility to take the reins and engage the company in this plan, as well as communicate and ensure the plan's implementation. Direction begins at the top, and this exercise will help the team members begin to envision their future.

The owner should allow the managers to lead but hold everyone accountable to implement the new goals.

Develop management succession.

Management succession is more than the replacement of talent; it is the development of talent. This is a time for the new team to re-examine and improve performance of the company's systems in a process of continuous improvement for the company's error-free productivity and profitability.

The new management team should develop the priorities and lead this process and educational effort for the entire company. It is a time for the owner to *coach* and *stretch* managers into champions, and for them to start thinking like owners and develop their team performance and execution.

Become a mentor coach.

Traditionally, you have strong managers who lead the company to meet deadlines and corporate goals. Now they must rise to a higher level of leadership, set a corporate direction, think like owners and build consensus. How do you change their behavior, build self-awareness and still maintain their spirit?

The owner evolves into a mentor coach. Management change is accomplished through the light of self-awareness, acceptance of the truth, peer evaluation, experience and personal coaching.

There are many processes and proven exercises to help identify managers' blind spots and move them to the next level. This is usually achieved through some type of "360" process that involves a review from their boss, management peers and those associates that report to them. This is an emotional process to uncover blind spots and is usually led by an outside professional.

Understand emotional intelligence.

Most of us recognize the term **IQ**, or intelligence quotient, from an educational system that heavily weighs this measurement.

Now researchers use **EQ**, emotional quotient, or emotional intelligence as a measurement. Studies have found it is EQ rather than IQ that is the key ingredient for leaders' success.

Emotional intelligence is reflected in behavior related to self-awareness, how one uses gut feeling, self-control of emotions, empathy, and the ability to inspire and influence others.

Give yourself enough time.

Time is your best friend when it comes to succession. Succession and behavioral change take time, and the sooner you start training, the better your results will be.

Understand the three parts of succession training.

There are three parts to this training: education, coaching and stretching. You will spend about 30 percent of your time with the first two—education and coaching. The key is to leave 70 percent of your time for the stretching process.

During the stretching process, managers are field-tested, apply their learning, make mistakes, adapt and mature. Stretching is considered the most important aspect of the process. Scars and bruises are great teachers, and it takes time to acquire them.

Coach the new CEO.

Every owner must realize their role with the new successor is to make sure he or she is prepared to lead the company. You must be a coach for the new CEO. Meet and decide collectively the process, timeline and curriculum for the transition.

Be OK with difference.

Remember, this process is all about the new CEO, not you, the owner. The owner's role is to teach, coach and ensure the company's future success.

The new CEO's management and leadership style likely will differ in many ways from your style. Let the new CEO find his or her legs and individual path. Do not intercede unless you anticipate a disaster in the making.

Learn to let go.

As the succession process progresses, you will observe your managers and the new CEO working more as a team and less with you. This is an indication of success. You will start to feel like a lame duck, and that is good news.

Eventually your phone will stop ringing, managers will bypass you and move directly to the new CEO, leaving you out of the loop.

The good news when this happens, is that the process is working as it was designed to and you have succeeded where most CEOs fail.

This will be uncomfortable and perhaps more emotional that you anticipated. You now must focus on life outside the business.

Notes

Chapter 8: The Final Word

—By Kevin Kennedy

"You must pay taxes. But there is no law that says you gotta leave a tip." —Morgan Stanley

At this point in your reading of this book you should have a much better understanding of the challenges that are before you as you plan to exit your company.

You are now familiar with the *three elephants* in the room that you will face during your exit: taxes, succession and envisioning your future outside the company.

You are aware that the entire process of exit planning can get bogged down with juggling advisers and the technical jargon of accounting, law, tax codes, estate planning, insurance and financial planning.

You might already be considering the key questions of your exit. How am I going to cash out of my business without being clobbered by taxes? How will I retire and not outlive my money or change my lifestyle? How will I replace myself? How will I find meaning, recreation and purpose in retirement?

And perhaps you are ready to take the next step of beginning to draft your exit plan.

To help bring these concepts into focus, I will close out this 60-minute guide with two real-world examples. The first will tell the story of a recent Beacon Exit Planning contractor customer. In the second, I will share how I would exit today, knowing what I now know from years of helping owners successfully exit their businesses.

Exit planning in action

In 2011, a contractor attended a two-day Beacon Exit Planning workshop in Chicago. After listening and learning from our workshop, he requested a proposal for planning service. He later informed us he was going with a local planner, and we moved on.

Five years later, he contacted us again for an exit plan. He simply said the local financial adviser gave him cookie-cutter advice in a canned report without addressing a key concern: reducing the tax burden and financial risk.

He told us that he had received a call to sell the business to a consolidator. I cannot share the details because of confidentiality, but a "generic" offer of this type in the contracting world would look a lot like this:

- A very low multiple offer
- A distress offer with little or no "goodwill"
- Taxes close to 50 percent or more
- A two-year employment agreement with a lower salary
- Sixty percent cash up front with the remaining 40 percent in a claw-back tied to the adjusted forecasted earnings, of which a portion is forfeited if the financial goals are not achieved.

In the end, the client was unable to meet his financial goals with the consolidator's offer because of the high tax bite. Additionally, the offer did not protect the careers of company associates who had helped him build his very profitable business. He walked away from the deal.

The client came back to Beacon hoping to develop a new exit plan—one that would allow him to meet his business, personal and financial goals.

His new goal was to sell to his management team and work part time for five years. During this time, he planned to get his team to the next level, then into leadership, and to train the next CEO to replace himself.

He was still concerned about whether the growing company's value and after-tax net would be enough for him to retire. But, the great news is the company's revenues had more than doubled since 2011, with a very strong profit margin. This owner is a grinder who will not be outworked by anyone, and the culture of the company and management team reflect the owner's work ethic.

To help this owner reach his goals, we used Beacon's proprietary DAD™—Discovery, Analysis, Design—exit planning process, described in detail in Chapter 2.

Discovery. The first step was to set up a series of conference calls where we interviewed the owner about his business, personal and financial situation. The execution and integrity of our plan must support the owner's goals in the exit strategy.

We requested a series of legal and financial documents for review to decide whether the structure of these documents accurately reflects the owner's intentions and goals as identified during our interviews.

Upon completion of the discovery phase, we prepared a preliminary outline presentation of our findings and suggested solutions for the owner's review.

Analysis. Once we obtained a thorough understanding of the owner's goals and objectives, a second step determined whether he could afford his plan for a management buyout.

Valuation and taxation issues related to his business and personal situations were a key factor in making this determination. Our report included a calculation of range of values prepared by Beacon COO Joe Bazzano, a credentialed business appraiser. This method is a cost-effective way to estimate the business values associated with the exit strategy selected for planning purposes.

We gathered pertinent information relative to his current business, personal and financial planning. The analysis in the report focused on the coordination of these three planning areas.

We found that our client was dependent on his business to support his lifestyle. He had been a good saver but was still too dependent on the business to retire without changing his present lifestyle.

The report illustrated various bottom-line exit options (before and after taxes) and tools used to reduce or eliminate taxes for a bottom-line understanding of his financial future. We made suggestions and diagramed recommendations for protecting his wealth until the liquidation event occurs.

Design. Upon completion of the Discovery and Analysis stages, we began the process of designing and illustrating the exit options in our 70-page report.

The report illustrated several options for the management buyout. Each option had its own characteristics and costs related to taxes and fees. It further identified both short-term and long-term goals for the execution of planning.

The report, or blueprint, lays out the short- and long-term goals, which will vary for each business owner.

We had to update his estate planning, purchase additional insurance, implement risk management tools, begin the formal succession process and draft legal agreement. We also assisted him in finding specialists in each area of focus.

We then laid out our plan in person. We feel that an in-face meeting typically is the most productive. This contractor chose to meet at my winter home in Naples, Fla., for the plan delivery.

We always explain to our customers that the delivery of the plan is not the *end*, but just the *beginning* of an extended process that can last for three months or three years, depending on how long it takes to align all relevant factors for the best outcome.

The number this customer needed from the company for financial independence was $7,000,000 net (after taxes). Beacon found a saving of nearly $3,000,000 in taxes and a net of close to $10,000,000 for his retirement.

This client has a very serious business-like manner and was always in the zone during the entire process. At the end of our six-hour meeting, his manner changed, as the bottom-line after-tax results of the plan unfolded and harvesting of the business investment. After all his years of work, he finally could visualize and clarify his financial future.

In three years, his goal is to work half time, and in five years he will have independence, acting as the Chairman of the Board, reviewing monthly financials and meeting quarterly for the remaining five years.

Good planning always pays for itself. Now the work begins to get his seasoned management team to the next level.

After we presented his exit blueprint, we made plans the to visit a car museum and then tour the various exotic car dealerships in Naples to see up close the many Maserati, Ferrari, Aston-Martin, Spyker, McLaren and Lamborghini autos.

One of the owner's passions is automobiles. After a typical 60- to 70-hour work week, he goes into his garage and rebuilds cars. He drives a truck and a Corvette on weekends. Naples is a car lover's paradise, as exotic cars are everywhere.

At the dealerships, his mouth was watering. It was like a boy in a candy shop for this unselfish man who never splurged on himself, only on his family. But now one of these toys was easily in his reach. By the end of the trip, he was negotiating on a two-year-old, low-mileage Ferrari California Convertible.

If I had a chance to do it again

In the introduction to this book, I told my story of buying a specialty contracting company with my team and then selling and transferring the company to the fourth generation. We were so fortunate, as fewer than 1 percent of businesses ever achieve this milestone transition.

But despite our successful exit, we experienced scars and bruises along the way. We spent six years and more than $250,000 (in pre-2000 dollars) wandering down the exit path. And, we finally learned that cookie-cutter advice cost us *millions in taxes*. If I had the chance to do it again, I would do it differently.

What can you learn from my exit?

Set goals. We were three different owners with three different goals. Every exit plan should be structured in a manner that supports your individual goals by defining your business, personal and financial needs.

We received two offers from consolidators and another offer from an M&A broker. However, during the process, we recognized the risks when considering consolidators, including the loss of control, protecting our managers and a poor cultural fit.

Once my team had more clarity regarding our goals, we only considered an internal exit—either an employee stock ownership plan or a management buyout. Our goal was to pass the company to the next generation of dedicated managers who helped us grow the company.

Know the tax liabilities. As we've discussed throughout this book, the tax rate of a business transfer can reach upwards of 50 percent. Owners can take a number of steps to reduce those tax liabilities.

For our exit, we were a C corporation and paid capital gains and state income tax. When we exited, a C corporation paid 34 percent at the highest federal rate (reduced to 21 percent according to the recently enacted Tax Cuts and Jobs Act), and a percent of taxes at the state level, which varies depending on the state.

Additionally, any dollars that come out of a C corporation are taxed again to the recipient as a capital gain on the difference between the liquidating distribution and your stock basis.

However, we could have changed our C corporation to an S corporation. This would have eliminated one level of taxes, as S corporation profits are only taxed once.

We could have also realized tax savings by integrating our transaction to support estate planning. Doing this reduces estate taxes and eliminates the capital gains tax.

Use an exit planner. We could have used exit planners to assist in a more efficient in design and execution, but to our knowledge they were not an organized profession in 1998. After leaving the company in 2008, I entered the exit planning business after receiving requests for advice from my business owner friends and colleagues. I did not become an exit planner until I went back to school for two years for specialized training and certification.

As an exit planner, I am trained as a process consultant to move an owner's goal on to a parallel path that meets the owner's financial target, replaces the owner, and protects his or her wealth with a comprehensive, holistic result. We pull together all the scattered information to arrive at a conclusion in the form of a blueprint, outlining the strategies and paths that will lead the owner toward a desired outcome. We can then lead a coordinated process through the execution

Understand the risks. When you exit your business, you are most likely entering the largest and most important *financial event* of your life. For most owners, the proceeds from the business sale are the resources that will carry them into a comfortable retirement.

You need the best information to help you minimize risk, make the correct decisions, and understand your financial and strategic control issues to replace your income. This process protects your hard-earned wealth and legacy.

In our exit, we did not integrate our transaction to mitigate business risk with asset management tools. This is particularly important at this stage of the game. Owners should create a strategy to support enterprise risk in a manner that does not overburden the company and insulates assets in a manner that makes them free from attachment in the event of a frivolous lawsuit.

Creating a monetizing plan. Owners should create an efficient plan for monetizing the value of the stock. Companies can aggressively reduce the price to buyer and seller to provide lower taxes and financial risk and decrease (and sometimes eliminate) federal and state capital gains taxes for the seller.

Aggressively save for retirement. Doing so will lessen your dependency on your business proceeds by participating in aggressive savings plans that are tax efficient. You can utilize life insurance in a manner that provides tax-free benefits and mitigates financial risks. Additionally, consider asset insulation vehicles such as trusts or limited liability entities.

Have a blueprint for your exit. Do you have a blueprint and understand your risk? We did not with my exit. We were fortunate to successfully exit our business, but if we had a better plan in place, we would have saved a lot of time and a bundle in taxes. Having all the information up front is the only way to make an educated decision.

In retrospect, these strategies could have saved several million in taxes, put hundreds of thousands of dollars in each of the owner's bank accounts and saved the buyers and the company millions more in tax dollars

You only have one chance to get this right and the intent of this book open your mind to the process, traps and options.

BONUS ARTICLE

Leaving Your Business Legacy

Beacon was interviewed several times for this article in *Asphalt Life*.

You spend most of your adult life growing your company to set yourself up for a comfortable retirement. When the time comes to transition the business, many questions may arise as you prepare to take that next step, such as:

- How can I take this success with me when I leave?
- How do I cash out without being clobbered by taxes or changing my lifestyle?
- How far ahead should I plan for my eventual departure from the company?
- What are my options for perpetuating my company legacy?

Finding the answer to those questions is a process called exit planning.

Link: httpbeaconexitplanning.com/bookbonuses/

Notes

About the Authors

Kevin J. Kennedy

Kevin is the Founder and CEO of Beacon Exit Planning "America's Exit Planner™" and Beacon Mergers and Acquisitions.

Mr. Kennedy is a nationally recognized speaker, a #1 bestselling author, industry voice and thought leader for exit planning and succession. He is a co-author of the Amazon #1 Best Seller "The Contractor's 60 Minute Exit Plan."

He bought and sold a non-family company that transferred to the 4th generation. During his tenure the team grew the company from 35 to over 200 employees into an ENR "Top 20" Specialty Contractor that has been in business for over 70 years.

Mr. Kennedy's authentic voice resonates with owners because he truly understands the different choices, taxes, emotion and complexities of the exit and succession process.

Joseph Bazzano

Mr. Bazzano is the COO of Beacon Exit Planning and Beacon Mergers and Acquisitions, a #1 bestselling author, a certified public accountant, certified valuation analyst and a certified business exit consultant with over 20 years of experience in public accounting, valuation and exit strategy services to closely held companies ranging from $5 million to over $300 million and co-author of the #1 Amazon Best Seller "The Contractor's 60 Minute Exit Plan."

Mr. Bazzano is national speaker to business owners on exit planning, valuation, taxes, and asset protection that have shown business owners how to increase the value of their businesses by millions of dollars with exponential savings on tax dollars.

His presentation style is to take the complex subject and make them easy to understand by using examples and case studies.

Book Bonuses

20-Minute Consultation

Beacon will offer anyone who has purchased and read our book a complimentary 20-minute session.

You will be linked to a three-minute confidential questionnaire that will assist in our initial "discovery" and make our time together more efficient.

Link: http://bit.ly/beacon20minute

Beacon Tool for an Online Valuation and Value Drivers

The odds of selling your business are not in your favor. Only 20 percent of businesses that actually go to market see the closing table. It is important to understand and invest in making your business saleable.

The following bonus tool is being offered to you so that you can identify areas of strength and weakness in your business and how it affects it overall value. It can mean the difference of getting three times and five times multiples for your business, or selling altogether.

Upon completion of the survey you will be provided with:

1. A risk score that evaluates the strength or weakness of key value drivers
2. An estimate of value for your business

Link: http://bit.ly/beaconvaluation

Beacon Exit Planning's Five Most Popular Articles

- Interview: How to Retire by Replacing Your Income & Yourself
- Buy Sell Agreement Landmines
- Leaving Your Business Legacy
- My Managers Can't Afford to Buy Me Out
- A Successful Exit

Link: http://beaconexitplanning.com/bookbonuses/

Beacon's Newsletter (Free)

Beacon Exit Planning has thousands of owners who enjoy our short newsletter with 5-minute articles and timely updates on exit planning, asset protection, succession, accounting and taxes.

Link: http://beaconexitplanning.com/contact-us/

Book Beacon to Speak

Book Beacon Exit Planning to lead one of your regional or national educational sessions for contractor owners on exit planning for an inspirational story and educational content. Presented by a contractor for contractors for:

- Contractor trade associations
- Manufacture contractor councils
- Bonding company contractor members
- Captive insurance contractor councils
- Contractor benchmark groups

For over a decade Beacon has been on stage telling their story and struggle to over 60 national and regional audiences. The target audience are construction/contracting "owners" 45 years and older needing a plan for their eventual exit and retirement.

Every trade association and membership group need speakers to provide relevant educational content to their membership. Our presentations are formatted for 60, 75, 90 and 120 minutes to fit your time requirements.

We also provide more comprehensive half day, full day and day and a half day seminar.

Beacon's session on exit planning is co-presented by Kevin Kennedy and Joe Bazzano. The educational style design we implement to deliver our message is both a story and technical, that combine two different approaches to individual learning styles of the left (emotional) and right (analytical) side of the brain.

It ends with a case study illustrating to the audience the cost of making the wrong financial choices during the largest financial event of the owner's life... their business exit. The case study will demonstrate our tools that can result in saving millions of dollars.

The first part of the presentation is the story (emotional) of Kevin' authentic journey from buying and selling a 200 employee, top 20 ENR specialty contractor and the wisdom of his scars and bruises.

His introduction is designed to the audience by providing the story, challenge and risk in the exit process. A journey that many of them will soon embark. This genuine experience resonates with construction owner baby boomers who intuitively understand the challenge but stuck by the complicated process.

The second half of the presentation is by Joe Bazzano, who is a CPA, Certified Valuation Analyst, tax specialist and Certified Business Exit Consultant. Joe communicates the risk and the technical side dealing with the exit process including monetizing exit strategies, taxes, value building opportunities and risk management.

Exiting a contracting company can be very intimidating, both from an emotional and monetary perspective. Because the complexities in the exiting process will include coordinating a variety of professional disciplines such as accountants, tax advisor, attorneys, business appraisers, estate planners, financial advisers, insurance advisers, plus more, can overwhelm the owner.

This session pulls the moving parts together in a manner that will help the owner understand the exit planning process in a method that is communicated to the audience using simple, non-technical terms.

Our lecture style outlines the process, reveals the risks, pitfalls and the key elements to succeed. The most powerful element is our ending case study that reveals our "tools" in action to demonstrate professional planning and saving millions.

Contact: KJKennedy@BeaconExitPlanning.com

Beacon Contact Information

Headquarters:

Harford, CT 06105   650 Farmington Ave

P (860) 756-0791

Kevin Kennedy x1

Joe Bazzano x2

Locations:

Newport, RI

Naples, FL

Dallas, TX

Email:

Kevin Kennedy: KJKennedy@BeaconExitPlanning.com

Joseph Bazzano: JBazzano@BeaconExitPlanning.com

Websites:

The Contractor 60 Minute Exit Plan:

www.ContractorExitPlanning.com

Beacon Exit Planning: www.BeaconExitPlanning.com

Made in the USA
Las Vegas, NV
25 March 2024

87725361R00066